The Thunderbird Review

2023
Issue No. 11

The Thunderbird Review
2023
Issue No. 11

Faculty Advisor
Darci Schummer

All correspondence should be addressed to anthology@fdltcc.edu.

Cover art: Ziibaaska'iganagooday Bwaajigan (Dream Vision of the Jingle Dress) by Robert DesJarlait

Cover design: Kally Lane Muenster

ISBN-13: 9798376036754

A Note from the Editorial Staff:

Boozhoo! We are excited to share the 2023 edition of *The Thunderbird Review* with you. *The Thunderbird Review* is an annual art and literary anthology produced by students and faculty at Fond du Lac Tribal and Tribal and Community College.

We received a record number of submissions for this year's edition, and while it was thrilling to have so much work to choose from, it also posed a great challenge as we are limited in how much we can publish. We really appreciated all the work sent to us, and we look forward to reading more next year. Thanks to everyone who made our editorial process challenging!

We hope you enjoy the work chosen for our 11th edition and are proud to share the art and writing of our contributors. Many voices new to the journal grace our pages this year, such as Indigenous Nations Poets Fellow Halee Kirkwood, standout Minnesota writer and artist Rachel Coyne, brilliant poet Elena Cisneros, talented FDLTCC Dean of Indigenous Affairs Bushqwa'idahmooqway (Roxanne Delille), and celebrated artists Shaun Chosa and Robert DesJarlait, along with several wonderful students from FDLTCC and other area colleges.

We would love to hear from our readers, and any questions, comments, or correspondence can be directed to anthology@fdltcc.edu.

Miigwech,
The Editorial Staff of *The Thunderbird Review*

Table of Contents

Poetry

Creative Nonfiction

Fiction

Art

Contributors' Notes

Echoes
Roxanne DeLille (Bushqwa'idahmooqway)

I didn't always want to be a girl.
It was sometimes awful,
and the why list is long:
expectation, perfection, perception,
a few of the *-tion's-*,
disrespect, disregard, disgust,
adds *dis* to the list,
glass ceiling, male superiority and sexualized imagery limited
possibilities,
barefoot at the sink and babies at your feet postponed potential,
it was work hard, run fast, think quick, cuss like a sailor.

No. I didn't always want to be a girl,
so, I wonder how she snuck out?
It must have been my gramma,
who wrapped her in my braids,
or my sisters' fierceness
who sang her into reality,
or my mom whose toughness
made females heroes.
They made it OK,
they coaxed her, dared her, and let her just be.
And it was she, who became me, that moved beyond her
into the woman who carries fierceness gently,
whose toughness is now decades long,
and whose song echoes.

Jiibay Ziibi
Allie Tibbetts

The question of where one is from seems so simple on the surface. I'm from Minnesota. I'm from Cloquet, a northern Minnesota town that reeked of Potlatch growing up, kind of glum and gray half the time with winter slush. I'd rather say I'm from Duluth. I miss saying I'm from Duluth. I lived there so long, and people at least might know where that is. The association to the overtaking power and magnificence of Lake Superior brings a swell of quiet pride in my chest. The lake is one of my best friends.

Maybe I come from her.

My daughter says it's her lake - "Zaagi lake." I tell her it *is* her lake. But now I live on the rez, so maybe I am from there. I'm from there when I'm talking in Ojibwe - "Nagaajiwanaang nindoonjibaa."

But all of that is geographic, and when I think about it, I've left a piece of myself everywhere I have been. So where am I really from?

I remember reading all of our stories begin with our mother. Maybe I am from her, the simultaneously brash and loving woman. She is sweet and no-nonsense all at once. She raised five girls, and sometimes one can tell she has had enough bullshit to last a lifetime. One can also tell she loves her grandbabies.

If all our stories begin with our mothers, then mine also begins with her mother. I remember when my grandma died, and we were going through pictures, there was one of my grandma grimacing, her face set in a scowl. My mom commented there was the mother she remembered growing up. But that wasn't the woman I knew ever. The woman I knew sat patiently reading a book outside the bedroom of my sister and me to make sure we went to sleep. At her funeral, my sister's voice cracked talking about how the sun had been shining that day, and that was what our grandma was to her. She was love. I think grandchildren get the best parts of their grandparents.

Maybe I come from her.

I like to remember I do. Because if she loved me that much, surely I'm lovable. Surely, I am worth something. That makes me think of how one day I was driving. I was feeling out of sorts. I was feeling low about who I was. Then I thought of my name. I didn't think of my English name; I thought of my Ojibwe name. And I remembered William, my wen'enh, telling me what it meant and shaking his head, amused as I stumbled to pronounce it. But thinking of what it meant that day driving down the road, it slowly crept over me that if that is how the spirits see me, I couldn't be too bad.

Maybe that is where I am from.

Sometimes I don't like to think of where I am from in this life. I don't like to remember the dark paths I have traveled, the ways I have acted, the things I have done that make me feel a pit of dread in my stomach. Sometimes I'd rather think of where I am and who I became when I became a mother. This is the best version of myself I have met along the way. And that came from my daughter.

Maybe I come from her as much as she came from me.

Like with my grandma, if my daughter loves me this much, surely I am worth something. I realized when I had her I am worth much more than I ever could have dreamed. I must be more special than I know if this precious little spirit embodiment of pure love picked me to be her mom when she was up in the stars. That too, is both the simplest and most complex answer to the question of where I am from.

I come from the stars.

Luna
Daniel Walker

Sightlines
Cleo Ashbee

hands cover the eyes
sometimes happy to be blind
to where we're from
to where we're going
searching for our home
in the spelling of places and towns
in the shifting boundary lines
and the flattening of these hills
my heart knocks behind the clouds
my grandmother said
her grandmother said
trading anthologies for apologies
our moth-eaten woven record is
tying knots and counting seeds
this is how we multiply
this is how we continue
reminding us that
renaturalizing begins with ourselves
maps do not create divisions; people do.
as the last shadow dashes across the grass
yielding itself to the sunset
I uncover my eyes
ultimately happy to see
and my heart knocks behind the clouds

Infinite humanity
Cleo Ashbee

we are burning trees
we are stars fallen
every place we set our feet is home
our ancestry wrapped in sediment
our prayers carried in smoke
the land was given to us to protect
we are new morning light
we are origin songs
everywhere we go we hear them
our breaths following
our labor and devotion
these acts were given to us as ceremony
there is nothing final in this world
we are as sunsets
we are as deadwood
we are infinite humanity
as twelve kinds of fruit
yielding every month
this knowledge was given to us to speak

Excerpt from The Mickey Orange Series, Book One: Keira's Rise

K.W. Jackson

"You thought yourself a part, small;
Whereas in you there is a universe, the greatest."
--Unknown

Rockford, Illinois, 2084

The shower wrapped itself around her as if seeking her shadow. The water, the heat. The coil of steam. The bathroom lights out. The spell, cast. The dark helped her mind wander, test out her growing abilities. This time, Keira tuned into her extra-sensory awareness: it swelled into an eagle eye view from outside of her, with an almost physical throb and stretching skin. Everything she could see seemed to be a part of her. Eyes closed, she could see the light creeping under the door from the hallway. She could now see the hallway, the exterior of her bathroom door. The hallway was empty, save the pictures on the walls; those frozen voices. The pictures now seemed to float by her, though she knew it was simply her awareness reaching farther, stretching beyond the hallway into the living room. She could see the glass she knocked over when she'd tripped past the coffee table an hour ago. She could see the television's black screen. The locked door.

Her awareness now suspended comfortably in the living room, her mind began its usual game, concocting scenarios of god-awful things. What if the door opened, against its will, as an intruder tracked his muddy feet into her apartment? What would he *hear* right now? The shower. Would he know it was a woman in the shower? Would she want him to know? Would singing aloud suddenly be a brilliant idea? If she were silent, maybe he would indulge in his own sordid imaginings. He might envision her, pulsing in movement, waiting for his hands. Or, he might picture her crying instead. Crying because her lover just moved out. Crying because she was ravaged, bleeding, as if some fiend broke in there before

before him but was polite enough to close and lock the door on his way out. Crying, perhaps, because she knew what was coming, but was too 'woman' to run. And, while indulging in his fantasies of her shower, would he get just a little bit careless? Would he forget to pull out his knife before opening the bathroom door? Would he know the fate he'd chosen for himself, entering the home of a woman that could (and would) end him in seconds? Did he even know who she was? Was this break-in a mistake? Did he misremember the address of someone else's apartment?

She turned the shower knob to the left, felt the heat rise. Her awareness still fixed upon the door, she decided to humor her imaginary assailant, or whoever happened to walk by. She focused her extended energy into a limb of sorts, not wholly unlike a hand, with many more fingers. She turned the lock, then the handle, and slowly pulled the door open. She hoped to hear the door's creaking this time, even from that distance from her physical location in the shower, even above the hissing water. Could heightened hearing now accompany her amplified sight and extended touch? Apparently not yet. She did, however, opt to leave the door open, just a minute longer. Maybe those mud-tracked boots would enter, for real. You put an opportunity like that in front of someone and who knows what they'll do. After about 40 seconds, one young man walked by her open door. He paused for a moment. She held her breath. He seemed to be deciding whether or not to close the door. Had he heard the shower? Did he know a woman was in there? A moment more and he walked away. Door still open.

She left it that way.

Turning the water off, the silence felt fuller with the mist. She breathed it in, imagined it fog. Her awareness moved to the living room window. The sun had gone down. She'd missed the pretty part; now it was just gone. In the bathroom she reached for her towel. With her hand. The physical comforts never got old. Now wrapped, she walked barefoot down the hallway, enjoying the slight give of the carpet under her feet. She ignored the pictures on the walls, those frozen voices. She stood in front of the open doorway. Her game should end now. A breeze met her through the entrance. Her hand reached the door. She thought. No, she was sure, she had grabbed the door handle. But had her feet moved? Was she still planted just a step from the hallway? No matter; the door handle was in her grasp. Her grip firm. With more fingers than spiders had legs. She shrunk her awareness back into herself. Still several feet away, she shut the door. Locked it.

#

Making a sandwich was hard work tonight. She couldn't stop her mind from wandering, this time remembering that as a kid, sandwich time was family time. She and her parents had had a routine, almost dance-like, when they made their sandwiches together for weekend lunch. They each had their own preferences in bread and content, so they each made their own instead of one person remembering what everyone liked. (Which they had tried once.)

But no. Now was not the time to be thinking about all of that, Keira thought, chiding herself. No good thinking about family while she had a knife in her hand. Opening the fridge, she suddenly decided: *Time for a change.*

The grocery store was its own form of claustrophobia. All of these random people that never made eye contact, never touched her hand, asked about her mother. Just a bunch of bodies moving around, clearly not dead yet. Wandering aisles for whatever their tongues wanted and their blood pressure cursed. She decided this place would be better named Slow Die. But hell, she was here too. She wanted barbecue sauce. Only no one sent her the memo that there were as many varieties of barbecue sauce as there were of ice cream. And her mind wouldn't rest until she had looked over them all. Eventually she settled on one that sounded like it had some Indian flavor. Reminded her of Jan. And on *that* thought, she put it back. *Screw that.* She began perusing again—

Hey baby. Those legs. Slammin'.

She froze. That was someone's voice. In her head.

I been scopin' you for 20 minutes. You better not scream or you're dead. Her head turned left. No one there. *Nope, not that way baby.* Looked right. Just an elder with a cart. Then something like a laugh in her head. His laugh. But more like a putrid moan.

Walking through the aisle briskly, she made her way to the cashier. The first smile she saw tonight. Probably because it was near closing time. She paid for her sauce. Which sauce was it anyway? In her hurry she'd just grabbed one in front of her and walked away. She looked down at it. Cajun style. Relief.

Sitting in the car, still in the parking lot, she tried to calm herself. She had to find out who the hell that was. She breathed slowly. Extended her awareness outside of herself. Swelling, farther than she ever had, into the store. She scanned every corner of the place, hoping to see a face to match the voice. Perhaps she'd spot a smirk of some sort, a hint of self-satisfaction, or delayed lust. This was fruitless. These days everyone's expressions were basically the same. What about age? He sounded like he was 25 or so. She scanned for guys, read their body language for any signs. She had no behavioral training though. Not her forte. Finally she returned her awareness to her car, into herself. Her forehead dripped. She fastened her seat belt.

Her phone was buzzing as she opened the door. She didn't check it until after making and eating her (much tastier) sandwich. And then sipping a glass of wine. She'd have to ask Briggs about the head voice guy tomorrow. Mental note. Finally she unlocked the phone and saw three missed calls and a text from Jim. Not good. Jim never called about anything good. Keira specifically remembered a day that she had heard he'd gotten a promotion at work and when he called, she was all set to congratulate him, only to hear him talk about why his recent heart rate was stressing him out. She opened the text.

Jan in hosp. Call me.

Jim still made sure Keira was informed about all things Jan, post-break up. Or whatever it was. It was all pretty strange. He'd been living with Jan for over a year now, but he and Keira were friends since high school. So he was now a fountain of unsolicited updates. Calls and texts about things she really didn't have to know. Something about this one though. *Maybe I should call.* She'd keep it short.

"Hey, Key." He sounded hoarse.

"Hey J. What happened?"

"She fell off the balcony."

"Really."

"Yeah."

"She fell."

"On accident."

"The last one was an accident. You said."

"Yeah, I just said that because I was at her bed when you called back. Didn't want to embarrass her."

"But this time was really an accident."

"Yeah. She was drunk."

"Then that's just a partial accident." It was quiet for a moment.

"She wants to see you."

"Doesn't mean I want to."

"Key. You're letting the bitterness speak for you."

"I've had a weird night, dude. I didn't want to wait 'til I felt normal to call back."

"What happened? Are you okay?"

"I've gotta hit up Briggs tomorrow. Might have a new one for the list."

"Huh. Alright, I'll leave you to that. But visit Jan, please. She'll be here a couple weeks at least, they said."

"I'll probably come but not tomorrow."

"Alright."

"Bye."

Ending the call, she sat down. Took another sip of wine. While on the call, she was able to extend her awareness to Jim's location. He was definitely at the hospital. His voice held up pretty well though; he didn't sound anything like the tears coating his face. He didn't know she could do that. She hadn't asked him for details of the balcony incident. His face carried too much shame.

Time for sleep. She'd been making progress the last few months, with the length of time she stared at the ceiling shrinking steadily, 'til now it was only about 8 minutes before her eyelids fell. Once the eyes closed, all she had to contend with was her mind. Dreams got weirder once she'd begun actively practicing her abilities. It was both easier and more difficult to control what she dreamt about. On one hand, she could more directly influence what would haunt her that night—or more accurately, she could influence what would *not* come that night. She could regulate which beasts would remain snarling in their cages. So that was nice. The hard part was that with the deepening of her understanding, the more she learned of what she was and what she could do, more and more subconscious memories became accessible to her. She'd never imagined she could remember faces, scents and sounds from her first months alive, say nothing of the days leading up to her birth. She knew her mother far too well. *Good god.* Sleep was elusive prey that night, but lazily elusive, expecting to be caught. Keira chose patience, knowing if her dreams overwhelmed her, she would have the strength to wake up. That was her term for escape. For instance, she never broke up with Jan, moving out of her house and leaving her to indulge in her demons alone. No. She woke up.

Untitled
Daisha Bosto

Untitled
Daisha Bosto

My End of the Sky
Elena Cisneros

On my end of the sky
the moon is obscured
by clouds and I just
went out there
and yelled, "Where
is the werewolf?"
My dogs' confused
cocked heads
stared at me
in the porch light.

Good times.

Passenger
Elena Cisneros

I can sleep anywhere,
on the floor of a bus, a stranger's house,
in the closet, under the bed,
in the hallway,
the backseat of a moving car,
passenger side with someone talking to me,
another's' bed, hotel, motel,
even while driving but that was only once and his voice woke me
up, it shook the car like thunder.

The girl and the mutt

Elena Cisneros

There's a girl in the field, fetal position, ice around her eyes. In the distance an abandoned trailer and sitting on the porch a mutt. The mutt knows what happened, so does the girl, and for the past week, while she lies there, the mutt keeps her company. The mutt let her know he was a boy once, left in the cold like her a long time back, and now he finds scraps all day, more than when he was a boy. The mutt says, "Sometime during the summer the spirits come all dressed in blue. There's a place near a hill. They walk into it, make sounds like whistling and drumming, then they walk out and the storm comes." The mutt let her know that she wasn't the first. "Not too long ago a man came to the trailer, kept asking for water and when he got none he walked through the trees." The girl listened. The mutt said, "Look to the sky, see that one right there? That one is my mother, and that one right there, that one is a stranger. Both have kept me company. Those up there told me this. We are inside of her, not alone. We are inside, and we breathe life all the time. Even now, you as you are, breathe life." And near the road, the trucks came with their searchlights, the mutt yelled for them, and the girl listened.

House Fire
Acrylic on paper, 2022
Rachel Coyne

Preventable Fires

Acrylic on paper, 2022
Rachel Coyne

My Dress
Acrylic on paper, 2022
Rachel Coyne

Utopia

Sara Sowers-Wills

When we step outside,
the sun makes a racket.
Distant rain crosses sky
in a stratus. A sparrow
dive-bombs a crow
to save a motherless
black squirrel.
We stand to watch.

*

By the time I'm at peace
with everything I can know
I will be dead.
Or, when
I'm at peace with everything
I can know I am
dead.

*

Painted lady butterfly rests
on a thistle,
the one I didn't pull.

A Thing Is Whatever You Name It
Sara Sowers-Wills

Words repeated attract
themselves and their sisters.
So you'd better choose good ones
lest you want a bungalow
full of expensive spank
in need of finishing touches
euphemistic for "a dump".
See the fractal in the scourge—
choose intentionality and spiders
an infinite supply of legs
that build at your command
and then some.

Scour "and then some".
What's in that place—
and then some,
if not recursivity, ova, new
promise—if not dark
energy, a mystery, what
causes wood to rot
but moss to reproduce.
Is it really a mystery
or just a thing
we're not ready or willing
to see yet?

Repaint the scourge
to look like a sunrise
porch in warm shine
a two-person swing
coffee with Baudrillard.
Turn the day's dimming

into tart verse, a thing
of self-similar structure
easily found in nature.

Walk the Line Where Water Meets Air
Sara Sowers-Wills

I am a stick
person. I am
food for deer. I'm
rain on a tin
menu. I am
a thing stuck in
space-time. I am
indigo in
a hot canoe.
I am rocks in
a deep pocket.
I am ice on
the surface, held
breath settling
resilience in
ephemera
bright white in sky.
A stick requires
definition
so it doesn't
get mistaken
for a weapon.

In the Library

Julie Gard

Your lips are moving, but from the other side of the library, I have no idea what you're saying. You are speaking in Spanish, I'm pretty sure, which I've only studied on a phone app taught by a green cartoon bird. So I can't understand a moving mouth across a cavernous room in a former monastery where a saint on a pillar holds a tray on a head.

First I think you're asking a question about the contemporary artist who's the subject of this well-attended public talk, linked to a trenchant observation on sweeping landscapes and arte Moderno. On second thought, I think you're telling me, en particular, to be careful. Just here and now in Oaxaca City, or for the rest of my life?

If you knew me, you'd know that I always proceed with caution. But do you? From your serious mouth, burning eyes, and long ponytail, I can't tell. I know you live in a dream, by which I mean as a sentinel. As the talk winds down, the scholar's laser pointer strays from the set-up screen. The target of light on your forehead doesn't stop your soundless speech. Your air words coil around me. I imagine, for a second, your body curling around me.

The audience claps and you don't start clapping, which leads me to think you're not really here. But I'm pretty sure you've warned me to be careful—¡Ten cuidado!—so when everyone gets up to go, I weave with them obediently through the folding chairs. You remain in your corner, now speaking solemnly into a book. You will stay as long as they let you. You will say what you have to.

Night Watch
Julie Gard

I long to sleep the way I used to sleep, without this hour of disturbance at the silver sink next to the dripping dishwasher. At last we got to the bottom of it, why the floorboards warped, why the fridge was ringed with water. In an old house, it's all in the slope. We pried off the kick plate and watched the sputtering leak from the very center.

As I rinse the blue plates, trying not to clank, I meet my own eyes in the window. If my neighbor were awake and getting a glass of water, I would see the silver top of his head. Every night there's a sighting: at the sink, in his chair by the front window, in the backyard as he drags out recycling. It can take a whole day to find someone who fell, for them to find you.

But no one's falling now. Everyone I love is swathed in sheets, chests rising in rhythm. My friend in California has a motion-sensing, infrared camera that tracks raccoon babies and shiny skunks and possums with glowing eyes. They're up and about, like me with my soapy jars. Like me with my cracked lunch lids, rinsing off yesterday's acorn squash.

Then folding old, striped kitchen towels that soaked up inching water. In a pool of chandelier light turned to dim, flooding the dining room table piled with clothes, I work on a problem. Fold the bootcuts, fold the skinnies, match the socks that can be matched. If this then that, I whisper, stuffing dream drawers with towels. In the war zone, it's already morning.

Let's Start at the Bottom
Dani Pieratos

Let's start at the bottom
Of Maslov's hierarchy of needs
Food and Sex
Where political parties are thrown on top of our
Politicized bodies
Bartering us and commodity food
Seems we are just commodities too

At the bottom
She is marketed as cheap, convenient and reusable
Men filled with
Liquor
Lick her
And the rest is something we don't talk about

Awaiting the coming of the 8th fire
I inhale cigarettes
To fill myself with smudge
As if to cope
Systems now changing
Becoming anointed with hope
Let's pray it soon releases the grip
On all the women it's choked

Dear Mr. Prosecutor
Dani Pieratos

How do you explain to a prosecutor
The plight of the People
Epidemics that have all but wiped us out
Them not being our fault
Being able only to feel comparison between myself and a cockroach
The only way to get rid of me is to stomp me out
However,
I will be the ghost on your back
Whenever you want to think of Justice
I will spill more blood from my place as the thorn in your side
I'll be that ever constant and annoying reminder of rape and
ethnocide
Of disease
You find them encapsulated in me
The Defendant
On the defensive since colonial times

Prayer Poem to the Grandmas

Dani Pieratos

I think that my value system is just relative to the position I happen
to find myself in
I can see why religions had to write it all down on paper just to
make sure we were on the same page
My people we burn sage
I hear it's good for the soul
So good that they put it down on birch bark scrolls
But
We don't really read those anymore yet that's not to say that we
don't need them anymore
In fact
I pray to my grandmothers daily
Grandmothers come and save me
Otherwise, I am, subjected to the dirty lyrics of a rap song and all
they have to say is
Shake it all night long
Grandmothers
Though a 1000 years of hard earned, righteous learning had been
punched and pillaged out of you
I'm still looking for you to tell me what to do
Grandmothers
I am not on a mission for purity but for respect
I reached my hand out for love but all I've touched is neglect
Grandmothers
I know what I'm asking is simple
Albeit not easy
For now
Hold my hand
Stand me up
And dust me off

Star Child
Acrylic on canvas, 2021
Shaun Chosa

Why So Indigenous
Acrylic on board, 2022
Shaun Chosa

Wild NDN
Acrylic on canvas, 2022
Shaun Chosa

Dear Potential Football Player

Stephen Webster

Dear Potential Football Player,

It is with regret that we have to deny your acceptance into our athletic program. Although your film is remarkable, your grades are not. Well, let's say that we have seen better—much better. Maybe you can play for a school that accepts failures that resemble your GPA. Your talents on film are not duplicated on paper. We are not surprised though as we receive many applicants who are of color that don't have what it takes on paper. But your film is amazing! Your running and tackles can get our team to win games. Maybe next time. Who are we kidding? There is no next time because you will probably never look good on paper. Have you considered that maybe college is not for you? There are other possibilities. It is a shame that such talent is going to waste though. I wish we could help, but you probably would not make it here. We have reviewed your many recommendations from teachers and employers who speak highly of your character and work ethic and have taken serious thought to all the improvements you have made in your academics. Unfortunately, we don't accept students like you. A GPA of a 3.4 is not accepted here. Good luck to you.

With Regret,

A College Located Nearby

America, 2022
in response to Walt Whitman's "America"
Lane Henson

Self-centered fringe communities, alike
in their preference: red or blue on white
skin. Equity, equality - these are
words against capital. The old money
blooms each spring. Property. The once-green earth
is property. These laws love neither us
nor our voices singing in the streets. Mother
indeed. She'd as soon make that flag a noose.

Elegy for a Cottonwood Marked for the Saw
Lane Henson

From gravel I harvest this dust in my lungs,
name this stretch Lone Cottonwood Road.
October has crowned you monarch of yellow tremblings.
Your court is corn-stubble, wide and far
as the county line. Some of your faithful
are bowed nose-to-ground, most of them severed
by the combine's gleaming reel.

Like a searchlight on this field,
a cut of sun through gunmetal sky has emblazoned
the gold you'd pay to keep your head—
the house of branches where crows fidget and cry
when winter has spent you.

I circle you like a breeze,
sleep in the crook where your roots
ache into black dirt.
Though I cannot translate their currency,
your leaves falling brightly around me are coins.

Harvest
Andrea Potyondy-Smith

Mist mingles with low-
slung mare's tails on
the eastern horizon
this September sunrise.

Superior starts to
shed her summer skin—
sighing inwardly, shivering
with the coupled compulsions of longing
and regret.

Squall
Andrea Potyondy-Smith

White pines saturated
with heavy snow—

vanquished Titans bowed
beneath an alabaster burden;

grey clouds scud across
the sunless sky. All

is swollen with solitude
and silence.

At a Gallop
   - After Annie Proulx
Tina Higgins Wussow

I read a story about a tall woman telling a tall tale in a dark old bar
that stunk like hundred-year-old urine. Her body was all muscle and
silk. When she spoke, the man watching saw no human woman but
instead, an animal. A horse. Something bigger than him. Something
to break.

When she laughed, her nostrils flared, and she stared right through
him while she lied. Everclear electric fire flowed down her throat.

"The steer," she said, "was only half skinned, killed quick with an
axe, but only half skinned. Its tongue cut out for the farmer's
dinner. And that farmer, he was suddenly ravenous from the
relentless work of pulling hide from flesh, so off he went to the
house holding that steer tongue, his paws sticky with warm blood."

She smiled at the man across the room listening to her tale, flashed
her long white teeth. She winked a shimmery opaque horse eye,
knew his type, *like an engine with pieces missing, out of oil and salty
over it.*

When she winked, his jaw ached with fury and extinguished might.
*She got no right looking at me like that, like I'm a shiny penny about
to live in the front pocket of those jeans so tight they look painted
on.* That thought shot through his mind hot, right behind his eyes,
but he didn't say a word.

She kept on, "The farmer never had a bit of luck. Dead wife, drunk
son, failed crops. Not a hint of mercy, so he didn't believe in giving
none. That tongue, still warm out of the steer's mouth, was sizzling
in the hot oiled skillet."

She kicked her hoof, reared back and laughed like what she was saying was funny in some way. *Ain't a damn thing funny about none of her or that damn tale she's telling.*

Her lips parted again and she said, "It took some time to fry up that cow tongue, always does, but eventually that farmer was sitting down at his table looking out at the sun dried crops laying like blonde pubic hair across his field, chewing slow, almost like he was grateful, but if I said that I'd be lying. Then out the window, with his mouth packed full, what do you think he saw up against that mango sunset?"

No one in the bar spoke. She set her black eyes right on the man slouched and staring at her, tapping the heal of his boot steady like a heart knocking too fast. She waited for him to say something, anything.

But *there wasn't nothing to say*, so he set the glass of whiskey to his lips, closed his eyes, and poured it in, breaking her gaze.

"What he saw," she rolled on, "was that steer limping along the horizon, its hide hanging long behind like a train on a blood red wedding gown, its mouth gaping wide, something dark and wet trailing from its lips. And that farmer couldn't help but gag out that last bit of tongue he was chewing, could help it either that he couldn't tolerate another piece of meat in his mouth for the rest of his days, though they didn't number that many. After the curse of that steer, no one would step foot on that farm. The house burned, then the barn, then the farmer felt a pop up in his skull, right here behind his left eye," she winked again. "Pop." Saliva glistened across her lips. "That's what he felt and that's what he heard and that's what killed him, his brain drowning in blood."

She stood there tall at the end of the table, pounded her empty shot glass to the wood and laughed. "Ain't that something?" she asked the man who vibrated now with something, alright.

Something like hunger, like he'd always been empty.

"That's something," he finally replied. Looking away from her glazed oracle eyes, from the tremble of flesh across her cheek. *I'll break her, I will.*

She thought, but didn't bother to say out loud, *and this sorry piece can't even hold his liquor.*

Then that was it. She turned and walked away, flicked her tail at the nuisance of his grinding teeth, his piercing gaze. He was sour at her from the start. *Ain't no changing an animal like that.* Out the front door, the cool night air danced in her nostrils. She set off, first at trot, *not gonna let that piece of rotten meat see me run.* And then, once out of sight, at a full gallop.

Fire in the Sky

-Based on the Travis Walton story
Acrylic on canvas board 12x36, 2022
ChimakwaNibawii Stone

Chimakwa Bimose
Acrylic on canvas 36x48, 2022
ChimakwaNibawii Stone

The Third Ravine
Tim Moder

I walk among trees in the third ravine,
Gnarled, stately, weeping pyramids,
Each a door to a mystical city.
Rich Sugar Maples bookmark the century-
syrupy lips on fat brown cheeks.
I walk among trees in the third ravine.
I admire tan cones of the cedar in piety
while an owl in the night flies close to the ground.
Each are a door to a mythical city.
Squat, sprawling Yew do as they please
amid Colts-Foot and Horse-Tail and old growth Pines.
While I walk among these in the third ravine,
Bittern, Raven, Thrush, and Veery
rush through a Muskeg and Black Ash swamp.
Each is a door to a mythical city.
An Oak as an unopened book I read,
with the morning and evening star at my feet.
I walk among trees in the third ravine,
Each one a door to a mystical city.

Shrew

Tim Moder

Have there been fires and songs here
other than the certain slow explosion of morning
and the unexpected splash and cry
of a barred owl picking up a lean, wet shrew?

Gooseberry Falls
Linocut, 2022
Elliott Crompton

Tracks on the Creekbed
Carter Meland

First Woman is sitting right over there on that stump, you know the one, it looks kind of like a La-Z-Boy, chatting with Creek about movies and other important stuff. They are so deep in conversation that they are not paying attention to these crashing noises off in the distance. Trees are shaking and snapping, and getting all twisted and turned around, occasionally there's the sound of rocks and big handfuls of dirt flying around, hitting things.

These noises grow louder and louder and First Woman and Creek still are not paying attention until the noises get so loud that they have to pay attention. There's a high-pitched voice shouting, "Yippee-eye-yay!" It's a piercing noise, like a canine yelping.

"How rude," First Woman comments to Creek.

There's a deeper voice, rumbly like a V-8 engine, shouting, "Whoo-wee!"

"That does not sound good," Creek comments to First Woman and the words are hardly out of their mouth when they hear those two voices approach from Creek's opposite bank. The voices combine in a yelpy-rumbly way and are making a bunch of revving noises, "Vroom-vroom, vroom-vroom," until there's a crashing sound, like a vehicle smashing into a tree, and a big old spruce, you know the one, Creek's oldest friend, tips over.

"Timber," Spruce says as she falls. She bridges Creek, but happily lands nowhere near First Woman.

"Spruce!" Creek shouts. "Are you okay?"

"I'll be fine," Spruce says. "I was getting tired of just standing there anyway."

Before they have a chance to continue their conversation, Coyote and a friend come bursting through the brush above Creek, spinning and shouting and twisting every which way as they slosh down Creek's slippery slope, splashing through the now-muddied waters before skidding to a stop next to First Woman.

"Jeepers," says First Woman, "you boys play too rough. Don't you see what you did to Spruce? And Creek was so fresh and clean before you slammed through them."

Coyote leans his arm on the edge of the door, grinning. "Can't help it, First Woman. We love mudding, right buddy?" Coyote punches the horn twice and his buddy goes "jeep, jeep."

"Your horn sounds broken," Spruce observes.

"We love mudding," rumbles Coyote's friend.

"Jeep, jeep!" Coyote and the horn again.

"Still broken," Spruce observes again.

"I think you owe an apology to Spruce and Creek, Coyote," First Woman says and eyes his friend skeptically. "And so does your buddy."

Coyote twists his head out the window to get a glimpse of Spruce behind them. "Sorry, Spruce," he says.

"Thank you," says Spruce. "It's okay. I was kind of ready for a change anyways."

Coyote's buddy eases forward, making sure his tires are no longer in the water. "Sorry, Creek," he rumbles.

"Thank you," says Creek. "I feel myself clearing now." Their surface ripples, "But I think those tracks you left on my bed will be there awhile."

Red Squirrel scrambles across Creek on Spruce's back.

"See," Spruce says, "getting knocked over wasn't all bad. Now I'm helping the animals in a different way."

"That's a good attitude to take," First Woman says in that nurturing way she has. "Surprises don't need to be unwelcome." She looks back to Coyote and his buddy, "But sometimes they can be."

"But," Coyote whines, "I love playing in the woods."

"Me too," rumbles his buddy, but in a whiny way.

"I can't help it if Spruce got in our way." Coyote whines some more.

"Or Creek," his buddy rumble-whines.

First Woman shakes her head. "You two, blaming others for your behavior really takes..."

Coyote interrupts. "What are you two up today?" Coyote

thinks if he changes the subject that First Woman will cut him some slack.

"Well," says First Woman, "before we were so rudely interrupted." She gives the pair a hard look, you know the one, you've seen your Mom or your Sister give you the same one. "Before that, we were discussing the philosophy Bruce Lee expresses in films like *Enter the Dragon*."

Coyote jumps out of the SUV and hits the ground in a martial arts pose. "Man," he enthuses, "we love that movie, don't we buddy?"

"Love it," his buddy rumbles and crouches kung fu style, weight back on his left foot, er, tire. Crouches as best his chassis will let him anyway. Coyote and his friend proceed to face off in a variety of positions, squinting their eyes and headlamps, to give them that Bruce Lee hooded eyelid look all while kicking and chopping and yelling, "Hai-ya, hai-ya."

"Shaking her head, First Woman turns to Creek and Spruce. "Can you believe it?"

Creek mutters, "Not really."

"Me neither," Spruce adds.

"I know, it's cool, isn't it?" Coyote takes a break from his chopping and smiles, huffing and puffing, at First Woman and Creek. "We've really got some great moves, don't we?"

"They're better than great, bro," his buddy rumbles. "They are truly dank. Maybe better than the original."

Coyote blushes until First Woman asks, "Don't you think that's a little racist, Coyote?"

"Racist?" Coyote says, making his eyes all big and soft and as innocent as a caterpillar on a leaf. "It's just kung fu."

"Not the kung fu," Creek says. "The way you were behaving. All that chopping and yelling in some really distasteful 'Asian' accent." A disgusted ripple scallops across Creek's surface.

"And that thing with your eyes..." Spruce begins, but she can't even finish her thought.

"...is super racist," First Woman finishes on Spruce's behalf.

"We love Bruce Lee, though" Coyote says. "We just want to

be like him."

Coyote's friend rumbles, "We honor him by acting like him."

"I don't think so," Creek ripples.

"You're not acting like him," First Woman says, "you're acting like some sort of stereotype, not only of Bruce Lee, but of all Asian people."

"Bruce Lee looks like that, though," Coyote whines. "And he talks like that," Coyote adds like he's making a valid point,

"Bruce Lee looks like that," Creek points out, "but you don't, Coyote. Nor does your buddy."

"And Bruce Lee speaks his home language," First Woman adds. "Not some schlocky made up 'Chinese,' or whatever language you thought you were speaking."

"You act like we did something bad." Coyote pouts this time instead of whines.

"Because stereotypes are bad," Spruce says.

"They're racist," First Woman adds. "And acting Chinese like that is taking some peoples' real lives and making them into a farce."

"A plaything," Spruce says, "as if only your pleasure matters."

"With no respect for the people whose lives you're mocking." First Woman gives him a disappointed look.

"It's called cultural appropriation," Creek explains patiently. They regard this exchange as a teachable moment.

"What does appropriation mean?" Coyote asks.

"Taking something that isn't yours," Creek clarifies both their answer and their waters.

"We'd never do such a thing," Coyote's buddy rumbles.

"Who are you anyway?" First Woman asks. "You look like some sort of bougie Jeep."

"A very chi-chi Jeep," Spruce adds.

Coyote, happy to have something besides his questionable behavior to talk about, apologizes. "Forgive me my bad manners. First Woman, Creek, this is my buddy Cherokee."

"Hey, what about me?" Spruce asks. "You toppled me, remember?"

"Sorry, Spruce," Coyote says, "I'd never forget you." He turns to his buddy, "Cherokee say hello to Spruce."

"Hello," Cherokee rumbles.

"He's a big one," Spruce observes.

"Yeah, he's big and he's baaaaad and he covers a lot of ground," Coyote says. "We've been playing out in the woods all day. I bet we've covered sixty miles since lunch, eh Cherokee?"

"Eh," Cherokee rumbles.

"What do you do when you're not playing with Coyote?" First Woman asks.

"Oh, I get around," Cherokee rumbles.

"Man, does he ever," Coyote high fives Cherokee. "He's named after an Indian."

"A nation," Creek clarifies. "Not an Indian." Neither Coyote or Cherokee seem to be listening.

"What's an Indian?" Spruce asks.

"Oh boy," Coyote shakes his head as if he can't believe First Woman and Creek and Spruce could be so dim. "Indians get around, you know. And like Indians, Cherokee gets around as well. I mean Cherokee's been all over. The Grand Canyon, Monument Valley, Wayzata, Red Lake, up and down Franklin Avenue on occasion." Coyote slaps Cherokee on the back. "You've even been to Oklahoma."

"OK," Cherokee confirms.

"Sounds like a real nomad," First Woman says.

"Cherokee goes anywhere," Coyote laughs. "Just like an Indian. Put him down in the woods and he'll find a way out. Put him on top of a mountain and he'll find a way down. He's a natural at this Indian stuff, that's why he's got an Indian name."

"A nation's name," First Woman reminds Coyote.

"Sounds like a real farce," Creek says. They realize the teachable moment about appropriation has passed.

"Well, if that's a farce, then Cherokee's all Indian," Coyote says.

"Native-born American," Cherokee rumbles.

"A real child of the land," Spruce says.

"How do you find your way around so easily?" First Woman asks.

"Yes," Creek adds, "Coyote makes it sound like there's something really special about being a pretend Indian."

"There is," Cherokee rumbles.

"He's like totally spiritual!" Coyote tilts his head back and raises his arms to the sky. "There's something inside him that people who don't have an Indian name will never understand. It's like a global positioning system. He's connected and this connection moves him in ways you and I will never understand." Coyote lowers his arms and tells First Woman, "The French call it *essence*." He chef kisses with his fingers.

First Woman cocks her head skeptically. "Who told you all this, Coyote?"

"Cherokee did."

"Because he's named after a Native nation, he's an expert on Indians?" Spruce asks.

"Whatever he says an Indian is, that's what an Indian is?" Creek asks.

"Exactly," Cherokee rumbles.

"Ooh yeah," Coyote yips.

"So what kind of Indian things have you two been doing today?" First Woman suspects she's not going to like what she hears.

"Like getting so totally in touch with nature, First Woman," Coyote yelps. "Right, bro?"

"Too right, bud."

"You all should try nature sometime," Coyote enthuses. "It's so awesome."

"So I've heard," Creek says, but ironically.

"Sounds wonderful," says Spruce, but earnestly.

"Nature really recharges me." Coyote starts hopping from foot-to-foot. "We've been charging over hill and dale, hurtling over rockslides, scaling cliffs, and splattering through mud pits."

"If there's anything natural out there, we've gotten in touch with it," Cherokee rumbles, then adds, "We like extreme sports."

"We don't like extreme sports, bro," Coyote kicks Cherokee's knobby tire. "We looooove extreme sports! I mean the way we roared up that incline and skyed it over that old river back there, that was pure love, Cherokee. All natural."

"Yee-hah!" Cherokee drawls in a cowboy way.

"That doesn't sound Indian," Creek mutters.

"Pardon?" Coyote asks.

"Nothing," Creek says. That teachable moment is now so far passed that Creek thinks it might be orbiting Saturn.

"What's next for you two," First Woman asks, "some more getting in touch with nature, maybe?"

"I doubt it," Coyote says. "Probably something spiritual, right Cherokee?"

"Definitely," Cherokee rumbles.

"If I get real spiritual, maybe I can have an Indian name like him."

"Really?" First Woman asks.

"Really," Cherokee rumbles.

"I'd be proud to be an Indian like Cherokee." Coyote starts hopping from foot-to-foot once more, but then stops and gets all serious. "Proud to be so in touch with nature, and so, *so, so* spiritual." Coyote looks at his pal with deep admiration. "Cherokee gets me deeper into nature than you can imagine."

"I know, very deep." Creek ripples in that annoyed way once again. "Like the tracks he left all over my bed."

Coyote ignores Creek and starts hopping from foot-to-foot once again, as if he'd never stopped at all. "And if I'm an Indian, I'll get to wear some beads, right?"

"Beads," Cherokee rumbles.

"And buckskin?" Coyote asks as he hops back inside Cherokee.

"Fringed," Cherokee rumbles.

First Woman stares at the pair, baffled at their cluelessness.

Coyote presses the starter. "And have spiritual visions?"

"All the time," Cherokee rumbles, then roars to life.

Spruce shakes her branches, but is it a breeze or is she upset?

"Is there ever peyote involved?" Coyote pumps Cherokee's gas pedal.

"Only when Jim Morrison's around," Cherokee revs his engine.

"And sacred ceremonies?" Coyote drops Cherokee into gear and punches the pedal to the metal.

Creek tries to calm their quavering waters.

"Just like this," Cherokee roars, and his knobby tires spin huge divots of sand and earth out of the forest floor and sends them flying into Creek.

"Everyone should be an Indian!!!!" Coyote howls.

"Oh my," First Woman says.

Cherokee pulls out of a fishtail and he and Coyote roar off to the treeline and plunge into the quivering forest.

"Be careful around my sisters," Spruce shouts.

From deep in the woods comes the crunch and shatter of Cherokee into one of Spruce's sisters and the distant thunder of a tumbling tree calling, "Timber."

Creek turns to Spruce, "How sad."

"Wannabes," First Woman mutters.

Ojibwe Mitigwaki Nimiid (Ojibwe Woodland Dancer)
Watercolor (opaque) on watercolor board, 2022
Robert DesJarlait (Endaso-Giizhik)

Ziibaaska'iganagooday Bwaajigan (Dream Vision of the Jingle Dress)

Watercolor (opaque) on watercolor board, 2022
Robert DesJarlait (Endaso-Giizhik)

Giizhig Ikwe miinawaa Gichi-Mikinaak (Sky Woman and the Great Turtle)
Watercolor (opaque) on watercolor board, 2022
Robert DesJarlait (Endaso-Giizhik)

Look Here in My Eye!
Janis Fairbanks

The need to be loved and nurtured is basic to the human condition. This truth applies to all cultures. My story is but one example how love and nurturing influence a child. Sometimes one patient and loving grandmother and one adoring grandchild can cement a bond and forge values passed from one generation to another by simply spending time together on mundane tasks. My Grandma was in her sixties, and I was ten years old when these events took place, yet sixty-six years later, I treasure every word, every action of that dear woman who took the time to tell me stories and teach me things.

Grandma was born in 1895 at sugar-bush camp. She liked to tell the story of how her mother, my great-grandmother, was busy tapping trees and hauling sap when the time came to birth my grandmother. The other women in camp had prepared a hollowed space in the ground about four feet wide lined with cedar. Across the cedar pit the women had tied in place a tree branch that my great-grandmother could hold onto to keep her balance as she crouched over the cedar to give birth. Grandma was born, the women cleaned her and wrapped her up, and then her mother went back to work tapping trees. Grandma told me, "There were no hospitals for Indians in those days. I was born right there in the bush!"

I heard that story more than once and also heard in her voice the love and admiration for her mother that my grandmother had. She remembered that and other things her mother, my great-grandmother, had taught her. She wove those lessons into our lives as we went about our tasks at her place out in the woods by the lake in a small tar paper shack on the Fond du Lac Indian reservation. We had no running water, electricity, or indoor plumbing, so when it was time to do laundry at Grandma's house, it took an entire day, and we had ample time to talk. Gram and I did the laundry outdoors in the summertime.

Laundry day was an adventure all by itself. We had three

methods of getting water in buckets to do laundry. These were 1) from a neighbor's pump, 2) from the rain barrel that sat at the corner of the house, or 3) dipping it from Big Lake. For methods two and three, there was the additional step of straining the water through a muslin cloth to remove debris. It was a slow process, so we started early.

The laundry procedure was the same. We drew water in buckets to do the laundry for our methodical laundry task, which for a long time consisted of heating water on a wood-burning stove and pouring it into a galvanized tub with laundry soap to plunge the clothing clean. We did all the laundry in a washtub on the grass outside the front door. The close proximity of the washtub made it easier to haul the heated water from the wood stove to the tub. A good bar of Fels Naphtha would be employed to scrub heavily soiled clothing against the scrub board. We simply placed general laundry in the water and plunged up and down by hand with a plunger with a long wooden handle and metal cone-shaped head attached to it. After washing our items, we hand-wrung them and placed them in a separate basin set up next to the washtub. Next, we carried the soapy water in the washtub to the tall grasses in the field and dumped it out. Then we placed rinse water in the same washtub, dunked our clothes to rinse them, then hand-wrung them again. Finally, we carried the clean clothes in a basin to the clothesline to hang them up. We had a clothesline strung double between two large trees. Grandma had propped the lines up by long wooden poles with forks in them to hold up each line at the midway point. These poles were also used to push boats through the rice beds during the wild rice harvest. Grandma wasted nothing and often made her household items do double-duty. We used wooden clothespins and attached the laundry to the long clothesline to swing in the outdoor breezes to dry. Clothes smell so good because when we dry laundry outside, it is sun-kissed, and wind-whipped, and produces one of the freshest smells our creator gave us!

Since laundry day took all day, we stopped for lunch and dinner and took little tea breaks to rest. The entire process taught me to have patience and let things unfold. There's no use in complaining that something is too hard or that you just don't want to do it. It needs to be done, so just get busy and do it! There were times when the rain came before the laundry was dry. We could see that it was coming, so we took our baskets out to the lines and removed the clothespins, dropped the still-wet laundry into the baskets, and took it inside before the rain really started. When this happened, I took note of Grandma's calm acceptance of the minor set-back and learned to roll with the punches myself. When we hung it all back outside after the rain had passed, it dried smelling just as good.

Gram got a new house with electricity built for her by the tribe in 1972, but she never got an electric washing machine. Although it was easier to get water after she got indoor plumbing, she preferred using the same outdoor location she had always used to do laundry in a washtub.

I think part of the reason she wanted to stay in the tarpaper shack was because her husband had built it for her himself. That was another story she liked to tell me, about how my grandfather had built this house for her "forty years ago." Being there must have been a comfort to her by reminding her of him. My comfort is likewise heightened when I visit the old homestead and remember our days of quiet enjoyment using the washtub and plunger method of doing laundry.

We always did our mending on wash day, too. Gram liked to say, "You might be poor, but you don't have to be dirty or raggedy." She had a big button can that she kept handy for replacing buttons and snaps. She also had a good assortment of old buttons in the can from worn-out garments. I never got tired of looking at those buttons! They were various shapes and colors, and some had rhinestones in them. Working outside, the stones picked up the sun's rays and cast shimmers of light on things around us. Gram allowed me to play with the buttons up to a point, and then would give me little chores to do. "Many hands make light work" was Another one of her sayings. I must say, I did grow up with a strong work ethic!

We were always busy, but it didn't feel like work. I just loved spending time with Grandma. She wasn't lazy, not by any stretch of the imagination. She believed in work and in "moving your bones." She usually got things she needed for herself, but sometimes, when she had a lapful of mending to do, she would ask me to get the scissors or thimble or thread for her. Sometimes, I couldn't find the item she needed. So, she would direct me to the spot the needed item was located. If I couldn't find it, she would direct me again. I recall only one time that she grew impatient with me for not being able to see what she was telling me to bring her. She needed a thimble, and I couldn't see it. "It's over there on the shelf," she said. I looked at the shelf above the table but could not see the thimble.

"Where, Gram? I don't see it."

"It's right there on the shelf," she said again, pursing her lips to point in the direction of the thimble. I walked over to where she was sitting and put my head beside hers, trying to see where she was looking. Suddenly, she turned her head in my direction, put her finger below her eye and pulled her lower eyelid down, saying, "Look here in my eye!!!" I looked steadily at her eye until she released it and smiled impishly at me.

"Oh, Gram!" I responded, laughing. I went back to the shelf, moved the Baby Ben clock, and found the thimble.

Thereafter, when I couldn't find something, I would go to the mirror, pull down my eyelid and say, "Look here in my eye!!!" That still makes me laugh when I think about it, especially because my eyes look so much like Grandma's. It's a little technique I use when I get to missing her too much, because it brings her right back, sense of humor and all.

One time, Gram tried to teach me to knit. Her yarn was the color of cedar boughs, and she was making a potholder. She was sitting outside the front door on a little wooden chair, so I got another chair and sat down next to her, watching her work. She was always so calm and unhurried; it was restful just being around her, even when she was working. She spoke in a soft voice and sometimes used unusual words. It always thrilled me to hear the way she expressed herself. She said words like "t'isnt" for "it isn't" and "t'is" for "it is," which made it fun just hearing her talk. After I watched her knit for a while, listening to her explain what she was doing with the yarn and the knitting needles, she reached into her yarn sack and handed me a pair of knitting needles and a ball of yarn. "You can make a potholder, too, Jah-eence. T'isn't hard," she said. I got the yarn started, then slowly knit-purled my way through the number of stitches she told me to make before turning my needles to go in the other direction for the second row.

We worked leisurely, sitting outside enjoying each other's company, waiting for the laundry to dry. We took a little tea break, then continued knitting until we finished he potholders. We ended up with two potholders that were both the same color yarn. There the similarity ended. My potholder was about a five-inch square and fairly firm, while Gram's was a good seven-inch square and quite soft. I was already ten years old, too old to cry over something like that, but I sure felt like crying. "It's too small," I told Gram. "It doesn't look like yours!" I had tried to be careful, to not drop any stitches, and to make sure the yarn would hold together, but it was just so small! Gram took my potholder in both hands, held it up and looked at the work, then laid it down on top of hers. "That's just right to put a hot dish on," she said. "You knit tighter than I do, that's all. If you don't pull the yarn as tight, the knit will be bigger, like mine. You did good." She put little loops on our potholders and hung them in the kitchen side by side. It made me feel better that she planned to use it. I felt valued.

Gram thought it was important to be honest, too, and told me a story about her mother teaching her a lesson. We were picking through the spools of thread in her sewing box, when I pulled out a little spool, smaller than the rest, which had some bright red thread on it. Red is one of my favorite colors. I told her how pretty I thought that spool of thread was. She took it from my hand, held it for a minute, and then handed it back to me. I knew from the way she gazed over my head off into space, that a story was coming.

Sure enough, Gram told me about one time when she was a six-year-old and had gone visiting a neighbor with her mother.

Shortly after they got home from the visit, Gram started playing with a little spool of thread. Her mother asked her where she got it. Gram said she didn't want to tell her mother that she had picked it up from the table at the neighbor's house, but she told her anyway. "My mother told me, 'Don't you ever pick up anything that doesn't belong to you. That's not your thread!'" she said. "Well, it was a long walk back to that neighbor's house, but my mother took me back that same day to return the thread and tell the neighbor what I did. I never forgot that," Gram said. "After that, I wouldn't pick up anything that didn't belong to me. Not hairpins, or ribbons, or even rubber bands. If it wasn't mine, I didn't pick it up." My great-grandmother was a woman of principle and so was my grandmother.

I've learned that children need a routine and living with Grandma provided that. She also provided stories to instill values in me that I continue to live by. She taught me to pay attention to my surroundings by walking in the woods with me and talking about what we saw.

I learned that it's important to recognize that trees and flowers "do things" too, not just birds and insects. It's important to really look at things and recognize likenesses and differences. I learned early on the difference between a robin and a crow, an oak and a maple, a wild rose, and a lady slipper. She taught me the difference between "bird berries" and "snake berries" (those that we could not eat) and June berries and blueberries, those delicious berries that we could eat. The ones she called "snake berries" looked an awful lot like blueberries, so I'm glad she told me the difference. I could also tell the difference between the sound of an owl and the sound of a bear outside at night. Gram liked to tell stories about owls. She told me one story about an owl watching what children do. She said the owl always knows if you're not clean enough, and will come at night to say, "Who, whoo, whoooo's got dirty knees?" I always made sure I washed myself clean, so the owl wouldn't have to come and ask me that.

Another owl story involved a lesson that she passed on to one of her sons about not making fun of people. There was an old man who used to walk around the reservation, and as he got older, he began to wear glasses. The older he got, the thicker the glasses were, until one day, her son saw the old man coming and said, "Run and hide! Here comes gookooko'oo!!" (That's the sound of the Indian word that means "owl.")

Well, Gram heard him say it, and she scolded him right away. "Don't you make fun of that old man! He can't help it that he has to wear glasses to see! If you make fun of him, someday you won't be able to see so good yourself!" She had her own way of teaching the golden rule and the idea of karma.

We heard owls outside at night, but bears came pretty close to the shack at night also, and I could hear their deep moan-like grunts. They did sound a lot like hoot owls, but they were a bit raspier sounding. We didn't live far from the dump ground, two miles away, so bears were more likely to go there than to visit us. But on occasion, at night, they did come. Grandma told me, "Leave them alone, they live here too, so just leave them alone and they won't bother you." She made it known that animals have rights, too.

It was a quiet life back then, and I still prefer the sound of birdsong and rustling leaves to the noise of the city. We did have a tube radio that Grandma would listen to on Sundays, but mostly it was peacefully quiet there. We talked to each other or did a little reading. Before bedtime, she always read me a story. We went to bed early and she turned the kerosene lamp down low so there would be a little night-light for us. Her home was a tiny tar paper shack to outside eyes, but to me, it felt like a warm and welcoming haven in any storm.

I looked forward to Gram's stories. They taught me things, and I never felt scolded or shamed by her, just loved. She would tell me things from her own past and what she learned from her experiences. I appreciate having heard those stories and think it is an effective way to pass along life's lessons. When you love someone, the best gift you can give them is your time and attention. Grandma gave me that and so much more, all wrapped up in the nurturing she gave me. "Look here in my eye!" became my life's slogan for seeing things through Grandma's eyes. Lessons learned at Grandma's knee have lasted me a lifetime. Thinking of her and the time we spent together is still one of my greatest inspirations and comforts in life.

Dances for Her Grandmothers
Acrylic, 2022
Sam Zimmerman (Zhaawanoogiizhik)

Ezhi-dakonaawasod gookomis (The Way a Grandmother Holds Us)
Acrylic, 2022
Sam Zimmerman (Zhaawanoogiizhik)

Niwiijiwaaganag Maamawi (Friends Gather Together)
Acrylic, 2022
Sam Zimmerman (Zhaawanoogiizhik)

Gardens
Gray Zezulka

There will be
a time before you,
a time after you,
and a time between;
where our love grows
like wildflowers.
Poison ivy infests the
beauty and its roots
burrow into the ground
so I can never forget
the way that you loved.
So purely, so whole,
so filled with hope.
Weeds cannot grow
if we pretend they
don't exist, right?
Can't time last forever
if we wish hard enough,
if we throw away our clocks,
if we ignore the sun?
How many gardens
have I grown in my lifetime?
How many can I tend
before time leaves without me?

Untitled
Kiana Defoe

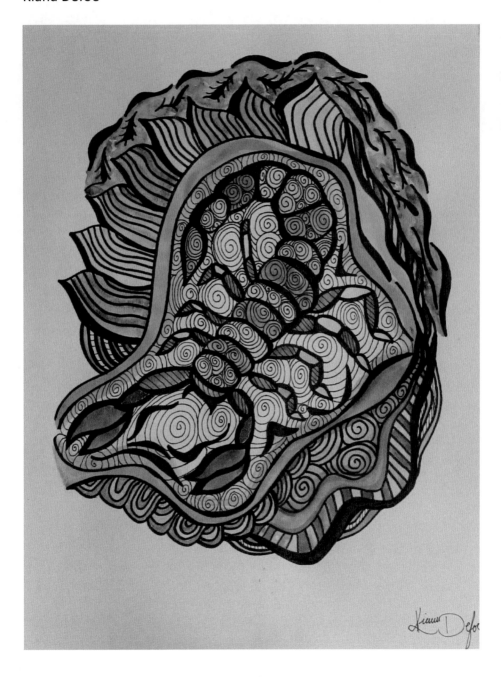

Battle of Motherhood
Ariel Johnson

I've always known motherhood as a journey of bliss, growth, and self-sacrifice I wanted to experience. I hadn't realized how much I wanted motherhood until I attended my 10-week ultrasound alone, due to the pandemic, and discovered my child was only seven weeks with no heartbeat. Children have always been a part of my life: from the time I started mentoring elementary students during my high school years up to becoming a teacher, I enjoyed teaching and working with children. Yet, it did not occur to me how much I longed for motherhood until I lost my own child in the middle of a pandemic that had disconnected me from the students I worked with and loved.

My bout with cancer at 19 years old had left me fearing that I would be unable to have children. I wondered if I had been cursed with barrenness and found myself weighing the desire to try again with the risk of losing another baby. I was forced to take abortion pills, since I was not miscarrying properly. The pharmacist's caution of "these don't mix well with pregnancy" still rings in my ears today. I took the pills hoping to avoid surgery, but I ended up getting a surgical abortion to prevent the infection from turning septic. It seemed my body was as unwilling to let go of my child as my heart was.

Still in graduate school, I tried to focus on developing the curriculum for my thesis case study through the darkness of losing my child. It was my chance to work with students, which was a glimmer of hope and something to mend my broken heart. I sat day after day under my dark cloud, envious of the sun in the summer sky. I waited for my chance to try again. Meanwhile, I had to endure the well-meaning words from people who may have been more supportive had they been lost for words: *Try again...it takes time...you're still young...at least you know you can get pregnant...* All the while I wondered if my partner would stay if I couldn't fulfill our dreams of creating a family as he changed from comforting to distancing.

Finally, after what seemed like an eternity, I found out I was pregnant again, and I was scared. Scared I couldn't protect the baby from my body, which I had loathed for not being enough from the time when I, myself, was a child. Scared this baby would be as silent as its older sibling at my first ultrasound. Scared the fluttering kicks would stop, never to start again. Scared the thumping kicks would come to a standstill. Scared to enjoy being pregnant out of fear it would end in tragedy. I tried not to think of being pregnant even as I planned my own baby shower and single-handedly turned what was an office into a baby room.

The pregnancy was mostly easy, with hardly any morning sickness. It was calm before the storm. Choosing to be induced to be on time for the benefit of others seemed reasonable, even to the doctor who approved the plans. My child was healthy. The doctor encouraged induction for that reason. My partner was expected to open for a well-known musician and having the baby on time would support him in following that dream. But when the time came, the baby wasn't ready or able to leave the safety of my womb and a c-section was the only solution. This was not how I wanted to bring a child into this world and doing so left me feeling defeated. I sacrificed myself, and almost my life, to support a partner who couldn't have cared less. None of this was what I wanted, but my wants didn't matter then, nor for months following my baby's birth.

The moment I first heard my baby's voice, it imbued upon my soul a beautiful, everlasting memory. So many overwhelming and joyous emotions poured from me in tears, just as raindrops dancing in the sun's rays create rainbows. But as the rainbow came to life, a bolt of lightning broke the sky as thunder rocked the world just as the words "She's lost a lot of blood" rocked our world. My baby and his daddy were rushed out of the room as I was rushed to surgery, hemorrhaging from the induction. The last thing I heard was that a hysterectomy may be needed to save my life. I thought of the baby's little face next to mine, clouded by the tears of joy.

I had a baby. A healthy, happy baby. That was enough for me, as long as I could wake up to hold him for the first time.

I'm not sure how much time passed or how many heart-wrenching phone calls my son's dad made to family while holding our baby close to his heart, hoping we would soon be together. With all organs still in place, albeit one stitched up around a balloon to keep shape, I was returned to the birthing center with almost three liters of donated blood pumping through me.

The next few days in the hospital were a blur. Just hours after leaving the hospital, my existence would be replaced by shadows, the entirety of my identity replaced by the role of being only my child's mother while those around me were idolized in the spotlights. My partner's dreams all came true at my expense while mine came crashing down from abandonment. I was constantly reassured that regardless of what I endured, at least the baby was healthy. Everyone took what they needed from me, leaving me with emptiness and confusion, except my baby, who deserved so much more than I had left to give.

I should have known something wasn't right when just days after bringing the baby home I was fearful of a summer thunderstorm. Worries rushed through my mind like the rain through the gutters. The list of "what-ifs" flashing in my head like lightning in the sky. My baby's father urged me to get some sleep, the lack of which increased my anxiety as I spiraled with rising and plummeting hormones. Though these racing thoughts and mountains of dread gave way to peace and joy after a few days, a dark cloud hugged the horizon as the storm front thundered closer.

The coming summer brought sunshine and adventures of so many "firsts." Sharing every moment together, it was just my baby and I and the world. But the world doesn't stop turning, life keeps marching on. From making a house a home and working to pay the bills, I felt constantly overwhelmed. I desperately tried to make enough time as I juggled everything on my own but felt guilty for every moment I had to set the baby down to keep the weight of the world from falling down.

Repetition became a close friend in allowing me to set my mind to autopilot. The days flew by as I coasted along, keeping rhythm with the ticks of the clock. My life became to-do lists, schedules, and reminders to help manage the chaos of work, motherhood, homemaker, and handyman on my own. I regret so much because the world was too much for me to enjoy moments of motherhood that I watched so many others experience.

During the day it seemed I was superhuman while carrying the weight of the world on my shoulders. But at night those storm clouds rolled through me, bringing darkness to my life as I was crushed by the weight of the world. I wanted nothing more than to calm the baby's cries because I felt so helpless. I'd cry softly along with him and pull him into me closer. I'd tell him that everything would be okay, and I promised I'd make it come true. But to this day I'm not sure who needed those words more: was it me or was it him? After laying him down in the bassinet, I would watch him in peaceful sleep. The storm would rage inside of me while I sat there alone. So badly I wanted to hold him, just to calm the thunder in my soul. I wondered too often what would happen to him if I were not around. What would his world be if I no longer existed?

Every night the storms would come, and tears would fall like torrential rain. Yet looking down at my Sunshine, my only Sunshine, the internal screams of loneliness and depression gave way to gratefulness. He deserved better and I had to be better for him. I made a promise to him that every day I would work toward being the person he needed me to be. Of all the storms I'd faced in life, this one was the strongest. A fallen home could be rebuilt, but now there was someone inside it. Yet I wasn't sure how many more nights I could face the storms alone.

Just when I thought the winds would knock me down for good, a familiar face with a heart of gold joined us in our home. My best friend, an angel with no wings, moved into our lives when all hope seemed lost. She held a mirror up to my face and showed me what I feared to see. But she took a moment to wipe away all the words I was told repeatedly. No longer was I "too much" or "too emotional." I was not "overreacting" or expected just to "forgive and forget" the gaslighting, isolation, belittlement, and manipulation I was put through by my partner, the father of my child, the person who was supposed to be there for me and for our child. A partner and father who, only months after welcoming our son into the world, announced that he never wanted to be a father to begin with and only wanted children because I wanted them. Behind my fear was something I needed for myself: appreciation, patience, room to feel my emotions, peace, kindness, time, and most importantly, forgiveness. Giving myself empathy helped me build resiliency, something that I needed to give myself hope and the power to choose my future for myself and my son.

As the days grew shorter and the nights grew longer, I was no longer afraid of the dark. My wingless angel became a sister to me and lit my heart with hope. I had a helping hand not only to help me juggle, but to guide me on my journey. Looking in the mirror, I recognized the person staring back at me. Instead of the shell of a lost woman, I had evolved into a mother. The title carries more honor than any other I'll ever have, though it took me months to accept this new title and understand my own value in the position.

In time I've learned to blend who I was with the mother I want to be. Though the journey isn't easy, I have my Little Mister by my side to bring the light of a million stars to the darkest and stormiest nights. I learned to reflect on peoples' behaviors: if I wouldn't allow that for my son, why would I accept it for myself? Although the role of being a single parent with sole custody is challenging, choosing that fate has brought me peace and safety. As I was told by my angel, "Bridges are burned to protect the villagers." A fire has the capacity to destroy, but in the remains, it provides the means to create. Just like seedlings that rise from the ashes of what once was a forest, I will build myself up from the breakdown I endured. A Valkyrie with a broken wing still has the heart of a warrior. A woman who brings life to this world will always fight the battle of motherhood.

Dandelions
Brittney Nelson

The young boy – kicking, screaming, crying
Another fit of rage
From nowhere it seems to come
Forever it seems to stay

The young boy – running over
Brown eyes shining
Grinning from ear to ear
Reaches out his short thin arm
A bouquet of dandelions wilting
Grasped in his little hand

Bimibizo Binesi (The Thunderbird Is Flying)
Acrylic on Canvas, 2022
Naakiiyaa Miskwakakake

Ode to the Underfunded Band Program
Andy Butter

After three bake sales, two bus transfers
      and seventeen hours on the road to Chicago
our ragtag team's turn on the wide stage
      of the Auditorium Theater.
Calvin has forgotten his bowtie but looks dapper in a crepe
      paper lookalike. Hanna has split the last of her oboe's
reeds and the whole trumpet section's embouchure
      is watery as gas station coffee.
Bill raises the baton and we bring our instruments
      to our mouths, no one thinking we'd get
as far out of our town, until we actually did.
      Others tried to answer the question of escape differently.
Two miles out of town Jeff stepped in front of a semi.
      If you stop and chat with him at the SuperAmerica
he might give you a free Snickers. David turned
      the shotgun on himself five minutes
before the Minnesota state baseball finals.
      The competition leers behind the veil of lights
wondering what noise we'll make as much as we do.
      Loathsome hawks. Well-groomed shark teeth.
Privately tutored and headed to East Coast schools.
      Under the weight of their perfect smiles we stand
a little taller proud for once to come from a county
      with one stoplight and who cares if you run it.
We blare our radiant jubilee, our panoply hullabalooing
      to the ceiling. Double forte like stampeding rhinos
pianissimo softer than warm butter.
      For more than a couple bars we were magnificent.
We do well and we know because even Jordan
      starts his saxophone solo on beat this time.
No, that's not right—this isn't the triumph of an underdog story.
      We misplayed nearly every note sounding at best
like a polite forest fire. Small as a grace note there was a moment

waiting in the green room, after Bill turned
the door's handle and before he walked in head hung low
with the judge's score where we thought,
no, we knew, we had a chance.

Address to Local Lords After Violence
Andy Butter

Dear Esquire of the Gates of the Arctic National Park forgive
the human heads skewered to poles. We did it to keep
the circumpolar north cool and up there.

Dear Knights of the Colorado River excuse the flood of human
effluent, our hollowed plateaus we filled with our bones.
Without soft tissue they make so much noise.

Dear Lord of the Franz Josef Glacier your lobed tongue caught
the chuff of our funeral pyres. Leave your answer
in a soon-esker.

Dear Baron of South Georgia Island you are an island with an
island's history, whale skeletons at attention outside
the abandoned Russian mess hall.

Lovingly, to Point Nemo's Jester, it's a trick to be alone like that,
equidistant from everything.

To the Viscount of the Eastern Iowa Prairie it was beautiful
here once, it's still beautiful but the shape of the bigger
beauty can be felt sadly.

To the Earl of Jay Cooke State Park under the shade of birch
a hot buzz of fly for corpses.

The Marquess of Grand Marais Recreational Softball Field
at best you are a grave.

With Regards to the Duke of the Swimming Hole off Fall Creek Road
water impinges, is poisoned, holds, is held by.

His Grace the Prince of the White Pine on 9th and Christian
      you were a center for children, their voices olly olly oxen-
      freeing to your rough bark.

To the King of the Tomato Plant on My Porch
      primogeniture's poison made need dangerous.

To the Commonwealth of Demodex on My Right Eyelash
      swaying beneath you I am bending with your assurances.

Entropy
Nick Trelstad

I know the folks
with white coats,
clipboards, and notes
have sold the sweet,
simple edict:
What is bad now
will be worse later.

But, they have only
seen the acorn fall.
Never the shell
crack, the roots
eat the earth.

Never the sapling
become hundreds
of hands, all upward,
reaching for home.

Dolls in the Window
Isabelle Hoida

Each limb was upbraided,
the uncombed hair—our harbor
from the separation. Two
slim bodies dangled in
our bedroom, oscillating, plastic
carousels my sister and I
knotted tightly together. As kids,
the windowsill was our
spot to scope out songbirds
and city scum. After the partitioning of
light and angles, we stared down
at the flower shop.
Noses against glass:
Customers lugged armfuls
of celebratory bloom to
ones cherished. We invented
stories about their heartfelt delivery,
our vicarious deliverance from
the flowerless, the fault.
Huddled behind the swinging Barbies,
we gazed at the shop door opening
and closing across the street. One
day, a man spotted our
spying between dejected limbs.
He was spooked—in his haste,
he adorned the parking lot with
a dusting of blue petals
distantly spread for us to
study behind the pane.

Blue Heron Water

Naomi Joy Nance

Untitled
Naomi Joy Nance

Untitled
Naomi Joy Nance

Fire Forest
Naomi Joy Nance

Absolution
Jan Chronister

On my knees
I crawl along our ditch,
pick out rocks thrown by a snowplow
or poured from sanders.
They nestle in dry grass
like Easter eggs,
some full size,
some pink quartz jelly beans.

Into the bucket I toss
chips of white limestone,
native gray basalt,
mica-flecked granite.
Each tells a long story.

This annual chore
cleanses me,
removes burdens
carried all winter.
I rake away dead grass—
green blades grow
into the clear air.

Zenith City All Dressed Up
Jan Chronister

She sits above lacy bridges,
Mesabi bodice
sequined with street lights,
hair pinned with towers.
Adorned with beach bracelets,
she smooths her blue velvet skirt.

We All Feel Heat

Jan Chronister

In hot weather
electric systems run on peak.
People with lake homes
float all day, cold drinks in hand.
In air-conditioned cars
they curse the price of gas.

A homeless man
on the sidewalk
begs for flip-flops,
bare feet burning on pavement.

Labrador Tea
Watercolor
Carl Gawboy

Christmas Card
Liz Minette

Hamilton,
our next door neighbors'
labrador retriever,
barks and whines,
his plaints soundtracked
into the early morning
frozen fog that hangs
like a gauzy fresh scarf
above where he's just
peed.

I am early
morning coffee,
writing holiday
greetings, as I hear
the scrape of door,
know it's Michelle,
our neighbor,
letting him back in.

I am writing "Merry Christmas!
How are you? It's snowy
and cold here. . ."
hoping maybe I'll get
a return greeting from
this relative who indeed
lives someplace
warmer.

Later I go to send these
and look for any Christmas
cards I might've received.

I meet Michelle walking
Hamilton.

Hamilton, who pulls
against his muzzle lead,
tread milling the snow
towards me.

Pulls Michelle too
into a brief December
conversation:

the winter bonfire
with beers, whiskey
Michelle and her
husband are planning
for this evening, their
Christmas card laughter
that'll brume above the
snap and spark of old pine.

But right now
all is Hamilton,
his thick muzzle,
like a whimpering
mailbox I take
between gloved
hands.

There are
no Christmas
cards today,

but this.

Flying IV
Oil on canvas, 2003
Diana Randolph

Returning to Their Source
Diana Randolph

Brown, bulging maple seeds
spiral and swirl, filling the blue sky,
falling upon the fertile forest floor.

Now, in late winter, once hidden under fresh snow
hundreds of maple seeds appear on crusty ice.
Blown through the open door
I pluck each one up
tossing them back outside, onto the old snow.

Their shapes remind me of guppy fish
that bulge and taper to their tails.
They swam in a large tank in my childhood home.
Sometimes I'd dream of guppies
propelling out of their confined space
to fly through our living room.
I ran around trying to catch
their spiraling, swirling shapes to put them back,
but I'd always awaken too soon.

I wonder if the guppies dreamed of journeying
beyond their imprisoned space, to their ancestral home—
the warm, fresh waters of northern South America.
Perhaps, like the maple trees, the guppies longed
to return to their source
to release their seeds, their eggs,
to continue their natural, expansive life cycle
in the fertile, wild world.

Making the Case that Every Relationship Ever is in Some Way Romantic

Jess Morgan

One of the most significant relationships as a high schooler was to the person you met with in the hall during the thirty seconds available between classes to stand by the water fountain before rushing to Spanish, or chemistry, or systemic gaslighting – I mean US. history – and in such a span of time, both of you needed to spew quickly the best gem from the day. And for the rest of time, you'd know that Water-Fountain William (or Bubbler-Time Brandon if you lived in Wisconsin) saw a water leak stain on the ceiling that was in the shape of "an animal if a zebra could have sex with an elephant." And although the word sex was still distracting because you were just learning what that was – at least kind of, because Mrs. Well-Meaning Wendy also skated over the details with as much avoidance as the entire student body did the lunch they serve in the cafeteria on Wednesdays – you wouldn't be able to look up at the ceiling ever again without feeling the same amount of wonder as you did the clouds.

Untitled
Elise Lehto

ages and stages
Meridel Kahl

she steadies herself
bows her head
of white hair
to watch her feet
shuffle on gravel

her hand
inches along
the side of the car
as she moves
toward a picnic table
on the shore

I stride by
in spandex pants
running shoes
arms swinging,
but stop short

as her image
catches in the net
behind my eyes

as shock measures
the short span
of years between us

Tansies

Meridel Kahl

Thirty years ago,
my mother and I
sat on a rock near the lake
surrounded by tansies,
their sun-button clusters,
feathered leaves
and waist-high stalks
rippling in the wind.

I wish this memory
were less dream-like,
more real. It isn't,
but tansies are.

Perhaps that's why every August
I walk the same beach road,
watch them sway in the breeze,
touch their velvet caps.
To some they are noxious pests.
To me they are bright beauties
glowing on rock-strewn shores—
yellow messengers bridging time.

The Place My People Go to Die

Sara Troseth

I have visited this place too many times this month, and each time I'm there, I am different.

This time I am going to live with my aunt while I attend college. The journey itself is familiar—a drive down a lurching, pothole ridden highway, curving to dodge construction work and forests, accompanied by a loud humming of tires and a sense of dread. Knobbled, stringy trees shoot up, bristles on a hairbrush, neatly sliced by the asphalt, and above the trees lays an endless expanse of blues and grays. My car and I can remember the drive by heart; my tires know each pothole and bump on the road, and my mind is empty, as if I was following an ancient migrational pattern. It's not long before the exit creeps up on me—across the bridge, past the concrete jungle gym of the casino parking ramp, and slightly right as the highway veers to a curve beyond the exit. Entering the small town, however, is somehow more depressing than I remember. A desolate graveyard of trees surrounds the pathway up the hill. Each one stands, brittle and frail as if it could topple from a slight breeze, without a single branch or leaf adorning the trunk. The grass is long, unmowed, and bent over from the wind, crunchy and brown.

My car whines getting up the hill. I do not pay attention to town when I pass, or the gas station on the way to my destination, or the restaurant I would eat at with my grandpa when I was younger. I try not to think of how different he is now. I just drive, glancing at fields, some loosely scattered exhausted houses, and road signs freckled with bullet holes until my car and I are swallowed by forest. Just before the road veers left, a gravel driveway and a pair of battered mailboxes reveal themselves.

In this place, there is a clearing hidden behind the giant bushes speckled with yellow daisies, but just beyond the signature towering toothbrush trees of the northlands. There are two houses; one, across the yard, is empty. Its single story is shaded, with overgrown grass and a lonely picnic table opposite a faded plastic swing set, the dirt driveway only used by cousins coming to visit or fix it up. In that house, my great uncle died. And in the years before he passed, his niece, my aunt, would walk across the lawn to take care of him.

The second house is well maintained. In the back, a garden of red willow, and sweetgrass, and large fans of white poplar leaves, painted a drywall-like color on the underbelly, creep against a fenced off dog yard. This yard, and this house, is a place of stories late at night when the sun dips behind the forest and the mosquitoes swarm the doors waiting for fresh meat. Unlike the abandoned house of my ancestor, this house is alive.

My auntie waited inside the house, busying herself (as I'd soon find she always was). She had given me boxes of beaded earrings the second time my dad and I came up here to help my grandpa move into a nursing home a couple weeks prior. I had not seen her since my uncle died. I barely remembered her or knew her until that day; my only other memorable experience was when she had sewn me a set of powwow regalia for my first (and only) powwow. My trunk opened with a thunk, clothes and bags nearly spilling out as a little dog barked endlessly inside the house. There I finally got to know her, a once distant family member becoming like a second mother who connected me to a grandmother I never met and a lineage I never explored. But still at that point, calling myself Anishinaabe felt hollow.

It had been about two weeks before one morning, my aunt took me across the bend. We carried four gallons of water with us that sloshed around in the battleship of a van for the three-minute drive. And when she pulled over and the van trailed off to a stop, the clearing was nearly silent. The trees did not howl with wind, and the blue jays did not question our presence, and the sky was void of any spots or clouds, drenched in a blinding blue. The sound of feet crunching on gravel filled the air, and before long we stood in front of my family's plot.

My auntie's voice broke the silence. She explained to me, nonchalantly, how each fallen family member had found their place in their grave. I watered my cousin's grave—he had disappeared after an overdose in the middle of a harsh winter, found in his front yard 3 months later. A gallon of water flooded the flowers over my uncle's grave, who died from a brain aneurysm, diabetes related. I went to his funeral when I had just finished stumbling through middle school. The breeze picked up as she explained each death, as if it were a fact of life and not the gradual, lonely shrinking of our family. Cancer complications, health issues, addiction. Two of her siblings gone in their 40's, a cousin roughly a decade older than I, a grandmother I never got to meet. I thought of the uncomfortable emptiness of my uncle's funeral, the hidden grief and love in my fathers voice as he called his late brother too stupid to take care of himself. I thought of my other aunt, bringing flowers to her son's grave who had stumbled to his yard in the dead of winter, collapsing under the weight of a fentanyl overdose. I thought of my troubled 14 year old distant cousin, knuckles bruised and bloody, abandoned by his father and trailing behind me like a ghost when we first met. I thought of myself, torn away from my origins to escape addiction that seemed to trail behind me, close enough for me to notice but kept at bay by my dad's, and my, determined resistance. The sunlight shone on each grave, reflecting shiny stones and gently beckoning the near-wilted pansies upwards. And brushing the dirt away, each headstone cool to the touch, I sat on the late summer grass and listened. My aunt had grown silent, but I listened. I listened to the land, and the stories it told.

I was not sad for those who passed—there comes a point where you become disturbingly used to the obituaries. Instead I thought of my auntie plucking weeds quietly beside me, who fought to reclaim peace in her home, who sheltered kids with nowhere to go, who swore off commercial tobacco and alcohol to keep her and her son safe. I thought of my dad, who moved to the Twin Cities with my mom to give my sibling and I a fighting chance, even if it meant setting aside the ties to our land and our culture. I thought of that same 14-year-old cousin's smile, how it slowly creeps across his face when I crack a joke, and the grass peeking through the holes in the steps of that empty house as if to welcome my great uncle home.

This may be a final resting place to those who came before me, but surrounded by death is where the Ojibwe in me was born. Each family story has taught me how to carry myself, to embrace laughter and let go of anger, to nourish the relationship with my heritage, and to break down the suffering haunting my family until it is just that–a story. I left the cemetery knowing, finally, what this place meant to me. This land is a patchwork quilt of dead and alive, quietly retelling the history of my ancestors. This place is a history of my family: a place where my people go to die, and a place where those who remain learn to live.

G-Life
Jehoiada Goins

March Madness

Susan Perala-Dewey

If you find yourself
wanting to walk away
needing a break from your own head

if you find the air unbreathable
like you can't get enough to yawn or
reach deep into your lungs

if you find the heavy weight
on your chest refuses to budge and
your blood thickens with every attempt to move

if you feel trapped by marbles
refusing to stop and roll to
one side of your head or the other
as if the planets are playing tug-o-war
and the Steelies are winning over the clear Peeries and
Tomato Soup, like Mercury, is stuck in the middle

know the Earth is turning and
movement will come and light will find you
hold tight to all that frightens you now and

know the days will lengthen and
planets will rise and the atoms in your
head and chest will balance once again

I promise.

~The Vernal Equinox

Deprivation of Life

ShyAnn Ostby

When the mourning comes,
it is like an armored shield,
a wall that slams close to your mind's eye,
denying any possibility of truth-seeking.

When the heavens release a cry so strong,
it darkens what was once bright.
Lying in wake are deceiving roses
who comfort the coldest of stones.

When you wake from the deception of your mind,
chasing and clinging to the false premonitions,
curled up in the comfy distraction of a dark euphoria,

you discover death tricked you,
took the biggest of hearts
and turned it into the brightest of stars.

Split Rock Lighthouse Sign
Acrylic on wood
Mason Martin

Always Room for Interpretation
Deborah Rasmussen

I'm pushing seventy-five
he grumbles, as though at it
for centuries, doomed
as the man in the myth.

That we're still pushing
is the wonder of it, I say,
shoulder to my own rock,
eyes on the summit—

no hurry to get there, not
even sure I will, but keen
to roll this year forward,
settle it among the others

then scramble back down
to see what comes next.

Lavvu at Finland, Minnesota
Digital Photograph, 2022
Marlene Wisuri

Lavvu Shapes - Repeated
Digital Photograph, 2022
Marlene Wisuri

Sin City
Jessica Penn

162 degrees—the dry heat hits different in that sin. I packed up my Chevy Beretta I called the purple people eater. So naive I was to follow you and let you lead my demise. So many quarters I spent pleading for a way out. The water was shit. The grass was shit. The carpet was shit. You! You were shit. God I would kill to have my 19th year of existence on this planet back. To look you dead in your ugly face again and tell you this is the last time. No more fear—dry my tears and flee to the mountainside. Fake life. Fake words, fake noise, false hope, so many lies. You! You were shit. That day. You know that day. As I picked up my clothing strung through the grass, I picked up my broken life. Sifted through the glass. 12 hours. 12 hours I wasted blood, sweat and tears—5 years I wasted. But did I? I grew. I learned, I prayed, I drank, I grew! You're still a baby. Still a child having more doe-eyed children, leading more humans to follow your pathetic existence. Those babies. My heart melts like my life did in that sinful heat to think of those babies. My baby. My other baby that was spared your vicious psychological thriller of a con artist life. But mine is smart. He will be influenced by the shreds of decency you have left in you. The ones that swallowed the reasonable parts of me. God, he is amazing. He will be amazing because he will be nothing like you. You died that day. And you continue to die over and over and over and over and over again. Until one day we will be graced with the truth.

Untitled
Steven Martin

Never Grow Up
Maddy Lawrey

You begin elementary school
so excited for the future and what
it will hold for you. You learn
two plus two along with how
to read and write, the proper
form to hold your pencil and
how to pronounce "the," but
that only lasts so long. Then
you begin middle school. How
disgusting! Nobody knows the
word deodorant or how to use
it. You have your first kiss; it is
not at all magical. It's that stupid
planned kiss, but it's OK because
you're in love! No, you're not. You
are not in love with stinky
Nate. You turn 16. The flash of the
camera at the DMV blinds you.
Now you can legally drive. Wow—
that happened fast! You get your
first job. You like it initially,
but then you dread going. You get
your first paycheck. You can buy
what you want, when you want.
This is amazing. Soon it's junior
year, one year left! School
sucks, it's hard, and it's so time-
consuming. But before you know
it, that's over too. You blow out
the candle on your eighteenth
birthday cake and look at that:
It's finished. You're all grown up.

Raspberry Train
Kelly McCalla

Today was a tough day for my boy.
He couldn't understand why
the Hartland train tracks ended in a tumble
of saplings, wild flowers, and raspberry bushes,
why the red berries were sour
and the black ones sweet,
or why, as he looked closer,
the tracks didn't end,
rather the berries and growth
just chose to begin.

He wanted to follow them,
like a quest for a cup of why,
or a single found word offered to satisfy a sphinx.
So we did the picking. Together.
"I didn't know there were black ones, Dad.
How did I not know?" mumbled my boy,
his mouth full of berries.
We picked, laughing together,
wondering together,
him about abandoned tracks,
me about the end of his childhood—resolving
in rapture, not red rusting rails—transport,
not trains.

He turned 16, six weeks ago
and while I no longer count the days,
I do count minutes like these,
where he is still a red raspberry,
a boy, not quite ready
to be eaten by the world
and yet even while trying to hold
back my breath and count,

as if holding in the air
will let me hold on to each moment longer,
there is a sweetness to the resolution,
to this moment in the fading light of this day.
It makes me smile.
Even though we have never been here
on this track, in this town before,
he has had me with him
walking on these rails side-by-side,
every day for 16 years—knowing too soon
I would have to let him disappear
into the bushes and thorns
and flowers.

Raspberry Train
Digital Photograph, 2022
Kelly McCalla

Lake Inferior
Halee Kirkwood

When I die,
let me sink

into the lake
beneath the lake.

I will know
that the northern lights really mean it

when their radiation blues
& greens dance deep

enough to reach me.
I am too certain

of my will to haunt
to be allowed on land.

My mother claims it's the weather
which gave her

Bipolar, then Borderline, going
from 70 degrees one day to a blizzard the next,

snow, yes, even on the Fourth of July.
I'll die soaked in weather

double rainbows, freezers full of hail
waterspouts & sun dogs

I'll bring it all down with me
to Lake Inferior

& I will finally know sleep

in the imagined hell of French explorers

sturgeon & sculpin will come visit me
I won't make them feel bad

about their sharp teeth or fear
of sea lampreys

we will celebrate our ancient largenesses

we will be rumor & murmur
of that something

that's been inside
you all this time.

The One That Got Away
after Treaty Beer Can, c.a. 1980's, National Museum of the
American Indian
Halee Kirkwood

Stop Treaty Abuse!
the white can states,
twelve fluid ounces.
Drawing of a speared
walleye & yes, I know it
could be worse. *True*
brew of the working
man! written on the
can's flanks, topped
with a slender flame.
Is this Lienenkugal's
long-lost brother beer?
The bent & bashed
bottom suggests rough
travel, but the fact of
its body suggests care.
This follows me home
& into winter, sits
with me in my brother's
ice fishing shack, where
we never catch anything
but are reviled for trying.
When we run out of
things to say, the can
says *poach*, the beer
says *bomb* says *stone.*

Left-Hand, the Ruined River
Halee Kirkwood

My love is for the watershed less commonly
$$\text{dazzling, clay-stained}$$
$$\text{\& sediment-bloomed}$$

writing herself

across my veins

Nemajitigweyang
Gichigami-ziibii
navigation built in the names

of our left & right hand rivers

the love line of my palm sutures
at Burlington Northern train bridge

where fawns nuzzle
bloodroot
in long & cool shadows

where my mother was once
quarantined in her car
pregnant with me

on the other side of the estuary

when fourteen train cars
full of benzene derailed
spilled the raw material

of plastics   insecticides
      detergents   paints

into that left-hand river
        which nothing could make
                me love less for

        I must learn how to love
      that which does not
guarantee repair

     My parents ripping
        through night & blasting
              Nirvana as though

the river sings to them

      come as you are
        as you were
          as I want you to be

           come

           doused in mud
              soaked in bleach,
                as I want you to be

the way I knew love was the way
        sun was thrown across the river
            like a thousand calling voices.

Contributors' Notes

Cleo Ashbee is an Osage poet and recovering New Orleanian. She spends her time in Eau Claire, Wisconsin. Her work has appeared in numerous places, including: *Dipity Literary Magazine*, *The Lagniappe* and, the podcast *Hummingbird Blink*. Her fourth chapbook *The Private Instructions of Ourselves* is forthcoming in 2023 from Hierophant Press.

Daisha Bosto is currently a student at FDLTCC.

Jan Chronister is retired from teaching at FDLTCC and now spends time on her own poetry. She also helps edit and publish work of fellow poets. Jan has authored two full-length collections and seven chapbooks, two of which were recognized by the Wisconsin Library Association for Outstanding Achievement in Poetry.

Shaun Chosa is a visual artist from Ely, Minnesota. He inherited his love of painting from his mother while growing up in St. Paul, Minnesota. After serving in the Marines Corps, Shaun moved to Ely, where he now lives, produces art, and works as a graphic designer. He has shown numerous exhibitions across Minnesota, including Native Son, War Paint and Indigenous. His works address a variety of themes, incorporating his Indigenous upbringing. Shaun is an enrolled member of the Turtle Mountain Band of Ojibwe.

Elena Cisneros is a poet living on the Pine Ridge Reservation. She received her BA and MFA from Hamline University. She is the author of *The Sad True Tails of J Strait: In which there is contemplation* (2012), and *Dark Stars* with artist Susan Solomon (2014). Her book *In the Shadow Country* was the winner of the (2018) Worlstad Poet series by Tavern Books. Her poetry has appeared in the *St. Paul Almanac*, *Sleet Magazine*, *Red Bird Broadsides*, Coffee House Press *Coffee Sleeves Project*, and the Minnesota Book Arts Winter book *Lessons for Our Time* (2012). She also was a finalist for the Loft Mentor Series in Poetry and Creative Prose in 2016-2017 year.

Rachel Coyne is a writer and painter from Lindstrom, Minnesota.

Elliott Crompton grew up in Madison, Wisconsin, and lived in both Missouri and Virginia before making Two Harbors, Minnesota his home. He studied history and design at Virginia Tech and continues to learn through woodworking, block printing, and writing.

Kiana Defoe is a student at FDLTCC.

Robert DesJarlait (Endaso-Giizhik) is from the Red Lake Ojibwe Nation. His watercolor paintings focus on traditional family life, origin stories, and traditional and contemporary activities of Ojibwe-Anishinaabe culture. His commissioned illustrations include American Indian education programs and organizations in Minnesota. Robert is listed in Reference Encyclopedia of the American Indian.

Roxanne DeLille Bushqwa'idahmooqway indaago. (The sound of thunder is how I'm known to the spirit). Roxanne DeLille indizhnaakawz zhaagaanaashiimowin (Roxanne DeLille is what I am known as in this foreign language). Waabizheshii indoodem (I am a member of the Martin clan). Mushkaaziibing indoonjaabaa (I am from Bad River, Wisconsin). Nagaachiwaanong gabegikindaasowigamig indaanoki, Cloquet, Minnesota indaa. (I work at Fond du Lac Tribal and Community College in Cloquet, Minnesota). Bushqwa'idahmooqway is a mother, grandmother, auntie and active community member. Oldest of 10 children, she is very much a contemporary Anishinaabe woman whose life has been divided between reservation and urban areas. Much the same, her education has been divided between the traditional teachings of her people and mainstream education. She is currently the Dean of Indigenous and Academic Affairs at Fond du Lac Tribal and Community College in Cloquet, Minnesota, USA, where she was previously a faculty member and taught Communication Studies (Interpersonal/Intercultural Communication) and American Indian Studies for over 20 years. As Dean, she oversees Anishinaabeg Gikindaasowinan (the People's way of knowing) programs. She also is an independent consultant, professionally specializing in leadership and relationship dynamics; and, as a spiritual consultant, she provides numerous ceremonies for the community.

Janis Fairbanks lives in Cloquet with her husband. She creates stories to capture history from an Indigenous perspective and to encourage strong human values among all people. She is active with the local Cloquet writers' group. Fairbanks is a member of the Fond du Lac Band of Lake Superior Chippewa.

Julie Gard's prose poetry collection *I Think I Know You* was recently released by FutureCycle Press. *Home Studies* (New Rivers Press) was a finalist for the Minnesota Book Award, and additional publications include *Scrap: On Louise Nevelson* (Ravenna Press) and two chapbooks. She lives in Duluth, Minnesota and teaches writing at the University of Wisconsin-Superior.

Carl Gawboy has been researching and painting life in the Northland for more than 60 years. Born in Cloquet, MN to a Finnish mother and Ojibwe father, Carl is a member of the Boise Fort Band. His work can be found in museums, businesses, and homes in the region and beyond. The comics included in *The Thunderbird Review* are from an in-progress graphic novel about the history of the fur trade from pre-colonization to modern times.

Jahoiada Goins is currently a student at FDLTCC.

Lane Henson is a writer of poetry living in Duluth, MN. His words have recently been published in *Oakwood, Great Lakes Review,* and *Midwest Quarterly.*

Tina Higgins Wussow is a writer, teacher, baker, bookseller, hiker, and happiness seeker living on the Hillside of Duluth with her husband, two extraordinary dogs, a "keeper" goldfish, and possibly too many snails.

Isabelle Hoida is a senior at the University of Wisconsin – Superior studying Writing and English. She spends her free time dancing hiking, reading, collaging, and pampering her Corgi-mix Leo. Post-graduation, she plans to travel around the world and write about her experiences interacting with different cultures.

K.W. Jackson is a writer, dancer and musician. K.W. has been a recipient of generous grants, including the 2019 Jerome Artist Fellowship and 2022 McKnight Fellowship in Writing. K.W.'s poetry book, *Any Psalm You Want*, was published with Write Bloody Publishing in the spring of 2013.

Ariel Johnson grew up in Wisconsin and earned her Bachelor of Science from UW-Superior. After graduating, Ariel taught science at the Fond du Lac Ojibwe School while pursuing her Master of Education. Her love of nature has inspired her writing, photography, and curriculum business. Ariel has worked at FDLTCC since 2019.

Meridel Kahl retired in 2013 after 45 years of teaching. She spent the last 27 years of her career at The College of St. Scholastica in Duluth, Minnesota. She discovered poetry late in life and is grateful for the daily inspiration she finds in the many moods of Lake Superior. Her poems have appeared in *WritersRead, The Talking Stick, The Peninsula Pulse, Amethyst and Agate: Poems of Lake Superior, The Thunderbird Review, The Avocet, Bramble, Leaves of Peace,* and *Bringing Joy.*

Halee Kirkwood grew up in Superior, WI, and now work as a teaching artist and bookseller at Birchbark Books & Native Arts in Minneapolis. They are a 2022 Indigenous Nations Poets fellow, a 2019-2020 Loft Mentor Series Fellow, and a recipient of a 2022 Minnesota State Arts Board Creative Support grant. Kirkwood is the winner of the 2022 James Welch Prize for Indigenous Artists, published with Poetry Northwest. Their work can be found in Poetry Magazine, Poem-A-Day, Water~Stone Review, and others. They are a direct descendant of the Fond du Lac Band of Lake Superior Ojibwe.

Maddy Lawrey is a senior at Cloquet high school as well as a full time PSEO student at FDL- community college. Maddy is planning to major in psychology in the fall of 2023 in North Dakota. She enjoys caring for her three cats and dog and writing in her free time.

Mason Martin is a Philosophy and Sociology instructor at FDLTCC. He is married to Danielle Fagen with 4 beautiful children. He currently is exploring many different hobbies and passions from painting to making wooden spoons.

Naakiiyaa Miskwakakake is a mother, wife, and artist. She is a great lakes Ojibwe descendant and enrollee of RRFN band of Ojibwe. She is also a direct descendant of Matoaka Powhatan through her first child Ka'Okee Japasaw of the Powhatan (Pamunkey) and Potowomak Tribes. She was born and predominantly raised in Duluth but attended College in San Diego, California.

Steven Martin is 19 years old and a current student at FDLTCC. He is mostly inspired by surrealist art, digital art, and collage art. He mostly draws surreal landscapes, but during his time at FDLTCC, he has started to transition to classical Greek inspired drawings of people.

Kelly McCalla grew up on the Cuyuna Range of Minnesota. He currently serves as an administrator at Fond du Lac Tribal and Community College, has two young adult children, and he spends his quiet spaces between hours exploring and looking for moments about which to write.

Carter Meland is a writer of Irish, Norwegian, and White Earth Anishinaabe heritage. He takes writing seriously, but tries to do so with good humor. By day he teaches students in American Indian Studies at the University of Minnesota-Duluth about the wicked smart, moving, and profound things that Native writers have to say about the world and by night he tries to rise to the standards they set. His novel *Stories for a Lost Child* was a finalist for a 2018 Minnesota Book Award in the Novel and Short Story category.

Liz Minette walks a lot and this helps with her writing process. Some places her poems have found homes are Chiron Review, Earth's Daughters, and she currently has a poem on tour with the 2023 North Dakota Human Rights Arts Festival. Sometimes her poem sends postcards.

Tim Moder is a poet living in northern Wisconsin. He is a member of Lake Superior Writers and The Bad River Band of Lake Superior Chippewa. His poems have appeared in *The Sinking City Review*, *The Coachella Review*, *South Florida Poetry Journal*, *Paddler Press*, and others. Connect with him at timmoder.com.

Jess Morgan juggles many hats, working as a sound technician, patient educator at WE Health, contributor for Perfect Duluth Day, and photographer. They founded the Duluth Poetry Chapter in the area and have poems included in journals such as *The Nemadji Review* and *New Verse News*. Jess shares a Tik Tok with Henry, their "poet-in-crime" called @ColdLakeHotPoets.

Naomi Joy Nance is an artist living in northern Minnesota, she spends time wandering in the woods and fixing an old house.

Brittney Nelson graduated from Barnum High School and Early Childhood Development at FDLTCC. Her poem "Dandelions" was inspired by one of the preschoolers at the preschool where she works.

ShyAnn Ostby is 21 years old and going into her 4th semester attending Fond du Lac Tribal & Community College. Her poem was created from the depths of her heart and soul for a school assignment and she loves sharing it with you.

Susan Perala-Dewey lives in Duluth, Minnesota, with her husband and their Springer Spaniel, Loki, surrounded by the companionship and inspiration of the Northwoods.

Jessica Penn graduated from FDLTCC and is currently studying social work at UWS.

Dani Pieratos is from the Bois Forte Band of Chippewa living and raising 2 children on the Lake Vermilion Reservation. Her love of poetry started in high school and has been a source of comfort throughout the years to find meaning and purpose in the triumphs and tragedies in trying to grasp the wholeness of life.

Andrea Potyondy-Smith is a native of the upper Midwest who spends most of her summer on Chequamegon Bay. She earned her BA from Northland College in Ashland, WI, and holds an MFA from MSU, Mankato. She is currently a full-time faculty member at Hennepin Technical College.

Diana Randolph from Drummond, Wisconsin, paints and writes in her home studio nestled in the north woods surrounded by Chequamegon/Nicolet National Forest. She loves silent sports in all the seasons. She's the author of "Beacons of the Earth and Sky" — paintings and poetry inspired by the natural world. Please visit www.dianarandolph.com.

Deborah Rasmussen lives in Duluth, MN. Her poems have appeared on the Lake Superior Writers website, on Rattle.Poetry.com (Poets Respond), in *The Thunderbird Review, Bringing Joy: a Local Literary Welcome, Talking Stick, Barstow & Grand* among others. Her stories for children have appeared in *Highlights for Children, Cricket,* and *Pockets* magazines.

Sara Sowers-Wills teaches linguistics and writing at the University of Minnesota Duluth, where she writes and pursues research in language and cognition. Her poems have appeared in *Pleiades, Interim,* and *Denver Quarterly.* Recently, she and her husband collaborated to present poetry and music at the Planetarium on the UMD campus.

ChimakwaNibawii Stone is a self-taught artist from northern Wisconsin. He creates art that reflects the environment, modern life, and some elements of traditional storytelling. Recent work is currently on display with the 63rd Arrowhead Biennial exhibition.

Allie Tibbetts is from Fond du Lac Reservation, where the water stops. Ajijaak odoodeman. Allie belongs to the crane clan. Allie is both a teacher and a student of education. She is a mother, daughter, sister, auntie, runner, and paddleboarder extraordinaire.

Nick Trelstad is a poet and English teacher from Northern Minnesota. He has had many poems appear in a variety of literary magazines, anthologies, and journals in his short career as a writer. He is the author of one poetry collection, entitled *A Threshold We Carry.*

Sara Troseth is a Fond du Lac descendant raised in the Twin Cities area. Currently, she is pursuing a Bachelor of Science in Computer Science at the University of Minnesota Duluth. She is also a member of UMD's Indigenous Student Organization and recently began exploring personal heritage through creative writing.

Daniel Walker is a 31-year-old student at FDLTCC from Thunder Bay, Ontario, Canada.

Marlene Wisuri is a visual artist, educator, and co-author of several books on immigration, Ojibwe history and culture, and local history. Her artwork has been featured in numerous exhibits nationally and internationally. She is the current chair of the Sami Cultural Center of North America. She lives and works on the North Shore of Lake Superior where she often finds the inspiration for her work.

Gray Zezulka is an avid reader and writer who loves to escape into fantasy as often as they can. Drawing from their own experiences, they shed a light on mental illness in their writing. When they are not writing, you could typically find them researching the strange and unusual things that go on in this world of ours. They are currently in school for their A.A. degree, and once completed they intend to obtain their Bachelor's degree.

Sam Zimmerman (Zhaawanoogiizhik), a Grand Portage direct descendant, attended art school at the Rochester Institute of Technology and upon graduating he worked as an art teacher working with students with varying levels of disabilities. With his return home to Minnesota, he began to spend time with family elders to relearn cultural ways that he had either forgotten or not engaged in. With these new learnings and his desire to paint more, and use his gifts as an artist to celebrate, preserve and share Ojibwe culture and learnings which has included the illustration of six children's books for Red Lake Band of Ojibwe, publishing of a bilingual Ojibwemowin / English fine art coffee table book, *Following My Spirit Home*. His public art commissions focus on celebrating stewardship of the natural world and to serve to educate and increase the visibility and representation of Ojibwe contributions and histories in Minnesota.

Made in the USA
Monee, IL
30 March 2023

30599677R00083